Selma Burke

ALSO BY CAROLINE RUSSELL-KING

Do It Yourself Dramaturgy: 1,001 Questions to Ask Myself Before I Submit My New Play

Palliser Suite

Strategies: The Business of Being a Playwright in Canada (with Rose Scollard)

Selma Burke

CARVING A SCULPTOR'S LIFE

A play by

CAROLINE RUSSELL-KING

and **MARIA CROOKS**

With an introduction by

STAFFORD ARIMA

TALONBOOKS

Talonbooks
9259 Shaughnessy Street, Vancouver, British Columbia, Canada V6P 6R4
talonbooks.com

Talonbooks is located on xʷməθkʷəy̓əm, Sḵwx̱wú7mesh, and səlilwətaɬ Lands.

First printing: 2026

Typeset in Minion 3
Printed and bound in Canada on 100% post-consumer recycled paper

Cover: *Portrait of Selma Burke* by John Schiff via the Leo Baeck Institute

Talonbooks acknowledges the financial support of the Canada Council for the Arts, the Government of Canada through the Canada Book Fund, and the Province of British Columbia through the British Columbia Arts Council and the Book Publishing Tax Credit.

Library and Archives Canada Cataloguing in Publication

Title: Selma Burke : carving a sculptor's life : a play / Caroline Russell-King and Maria Crooks.
Names: Russell-King, Caroline, 1963- author.
Identifiers: Canadiana 20250255480 | ISBN 9781772017151 (softcover)
Subjects: LCSH: Burke, Selma, 1900-1995—Drama. | LCGFT: Biographical drama. | LCGFT: Drama.
Classification: LCC PS8585.U785 S45 2026 | DDC C812/.54—dc23

To Selma Burke, with love

Faith is taking the first step even when you don't see the whole staircase.

—attributed to DR. MARTIN LUTHER KING

Censorship is to art as lynching is to justice.

—HENRY LOUIS GATES JR.
"Foreword," *The Anthology of Rap*

FOREWORD

In 2003 I came across a poster of Selma Burke's sculpture *Untitled (Woman and Child)*. I was struck by the humanity, the pain, the freedom, and the poetry in her work. Even though I was merely observing this sculpture in a two-dimensional photograph, I was curious about who created this masterpiece but never pursued further investigations. It took two decades for me to come across Ms. Burke again. On February 24, 2023, Theatre Calgary produced a one-night-only public reading of a new play, *Selma Burke*, written by Calgary playwrights Maria Crooks and Caroline Russell-King. There was a definite electricity in the air as I sat in the lobby of the Max Bell Theatre experiencing this reading. That energy grew to the point that I thought to myself, "I should include this play in our upcoming season." Fast-forward to the opening night of the world premiere of *Selma Burke* on April 4, 2024, in the Martha Cohen Theatre, where the magic and mystery of Selma came to life three-dimensionally through Maria and Caroline's play as part of our '23/'24 season.

Selma Burke aims to create an experience that is more than a biography. The play seeks to express Selma's worldview, process, and unwavering conviction that art matters – not just as an object, but as an act. Theatre, at its best, is an act of remembering. It's where forgotten voices are raised and where quiet truths are spoken aloud. The publication of this play allows her voice to travel even further – beyond the stage, into your hands. It is my hope that these pages carry with them the same wonder and urgency that struck me all those years ago. May this play challenge you. May it move you. May it inspire you to look again – at the stories we tell, the artists we honour, and the figures we've yet to carve from history.

—STAFFORD ARIMA

Artistic Director, Theatre Calgary

PREFACE

How the Play Came into Being

CAROLINE RUSSELL-KING
and **MARIA CROOKS**

I review plays, adjudicate, work as a dramaturge, and mentor new playwrights. So I work with plays in one form or another every day. I turn to visual art to close down my narrative-driven brain.

I started out wanting to write a play about one of my favourite artists, Mondrian. Then I wondered what women artists were doing at the time he was working. Through this research I discovered the wonderful Selma Burke. Knowing that as a white Canadian woman, I couldn't write authentically about an African American artist, I sought a co-writer. Maria had taken my playwriting class twice and hired me as a dramaturge for three of her plays. We discovered that our political views coincided, and as an added bonus that we only lived three blocks from each other – so we took the plunge and began working together.

We applied for grants to write the play, were successful, and began the research. This is where I fell in love – with Burke and her art. We exhausted the resources of the public library and the internet, and then we found that Selma's papers were housed and archived at Spelman College in Atlanta, Georgia. So we contacted them. Their archive was a gold mine of personal information.

We started constructing a timeline of Selma's life, which spanned nearly one hundred years. As we found juicy tidbits, we divided the research and the writing of scenes.

We followed the golden dramatic rule of *conflict on the stage in the present.* This was to be a show, not a tell. We wanted to focus on entertainment and not education. And we gave ourselves licence to dramatize her story, calling it a "flight of fancy."

We knew we wanted to write a drama; we knew we wanted a small cast. We decided that there should be two females and two males (one Black and one white each) to keep the play marketable for production. This eliminated certain scenes and provided an artistic boundary.

There are three types of theatrical conflict: person versus person, person versus the environment, and person versus themself. The question I asked as we wrote was, "What makes this play theatrical?" It was then that it occurred to me that the art had to play an active role. What a wonderfully dramatic way to show our protagonist having internal conflict and expressing it *with* her creations and other works of art. Of course the art had to communicate with her, so we gave her pieces the ability to react physically and to speak. Things became even more interesting. The genre was still the same, not a fantasy. The art didn't have autonomy; her works only came to life in Selma's imagination.

We strung scenes together, dropped some, added others, and did a lot of editing. We created a dramatic arc with the exposition, inciting incident, rising action, climax, and denouement. We had a draft read by actors, and we rewrote. We submitted the script to a provincial competition, and it was chosen as a runner-up for the Alberta Playwrighting Competition's Sharon Pollock Award. We submitted the play to Theatre Calgary and were thrilled when they agreed to give it a public reading in February of 2023 for Black History Month. Luckily for us, Theatre Calgary also wanted to give the script a week of development. Dian Marie Bridge from Black Theatre Workshop in Montréal was brought in to direct the four actors. As a result, we did more rewriting. The reading was a success, and Stafford Arima, taking a chance on a new work, offered us a slot for production in Theatre Calgary's 2023–2024 season.

Delicia Turner Sonnenberg was brought in from the US to direct our fabulous cast. In rehearsal we continued to add scenes, drop scenes, and add lines and rewrite at the behest of Stafford Arima, who is not only Theatre Calgary's artistic director but was also our dramaturge. We rehearsed for three weeks, and with the help of talented designers and a supportive crew, we opened to fantastic reviews.

The show went on to be nominated for fourteen awards, winning among others a Calgary Theatre Critics' Award for Best New Play Script and a Betty Mitchell Theatre Award for Outstanding New Play. Later that year we won the Canadian National Playwriting Competition.

Together Maria and I carved out our play *Selma Burke: Carving a Sculptor's Life*, and we are thrilled that our script is being included in the canon of such a prestigious press. We are indebted to all those who helped along the way.

—CAROLINE RUSSELL-KING

When Caroline asked me if I would like to write a play with her, I was surprised, delighted, and I admit a little fearful that I would not be able to measure up to the task. Nevertheless, I recognized that it would be amazing to work with such an accomplished playwright, so I seized the opportunity. We began our collaboration in the fall of 2020, while the world was trying to comprehend the phenomenon that was COVID-19. In a way, this play is our COVID baby.

I had heard the name Selma Burke but knew nothing about her. Caroline gave me a children's book on her. It was my introduction to this amazing artist, whose life and work should be more recognized and celebrated. As we began our work, we dreamed of travelling to the US to view her art and to do research among her papers. We were not able to do that for various reasons, so we did the next best thing: we contacted Spelman College, and they generously sent us electronic documents, which provided us with plentiful and invaluable information.

I have never co-written anything before, and the experience with Caroline has been positive and a chance to reacquaint myself with writing plays, as I had veered away from it for several years in favour of oral storytelling.

We want Selma to continue to live on stage. We hope subsequent productions continue to be a joyous celebration of her life and her art.

—MARIA CROOKS

PRODUCTION HISTORY

Selma Burke was first produced by Theatre Calgary in partnership with Alberta Theatre Projects in Calgary, Alberta, from April 2 to April 27, 2024, with the following cast and crew:

ACTOR 1	Norma Lewis
ACTOR 2	Christopher Clare
ACTOR 3	Heather Pattengale
ACTOR 4	Christopher Hunt

Artistic Director and Dramaturge	Stafford Arima
Director	Delicia Turner Sonnenberg
Assistant Director	Lennette Randall
Set Designer	Hanne Loosen
Costume Designer	Adejoké Taiwo
Lighting Designer	Tim Rodrigues
Sound Designer and Composer	Kathryn Smith
Projection Designer	Brendan Briceland
Movement Choreographer	Javier Vilalta
Intimacy Director	Anastasia St. Amand
Voice and Dialect Coach	Jane MacFarlane
Stage Manager	Meredith Johnson
Assistant Stage Manager	Jennifer Yeung
Apprentice Stage Manager	Brady Hillman

CHARACTERS

ACTOR 1 plays SELMA Burke

ACTOR 2 plays CLAUDE McKay; PAPA Burke; CHAUFFEUR; GALLERY HEAD; DUKE Ellington; Rev. Dr. Martin Luther KING; and art pieces – AFRICAN MASK; GENTLEMAN; and one of the ISLAND DANCERS

ACTOR 3 plays PATSY; HANNAH; MRS. RIVERS; PROFESSOR; White House SECRETARY; First Lady ELEANOR Roosevelt; EXPO HEAD; MARSHA; Frau KELLER; ANNETTE; and art pieces – MOTHER; SNOW WOMAN; LIGHT AND SHADOW; MATISSE RECLINING NUDE; BURKE RECLINING NUDE; FEMALE WHITE CLAY FIGURE; TURKEY; WHITE FACE; ABSTRACT NUDE; DESPAIR; PROTESTER; Statue of LIBERTY; NU DE DOS, QUATRIÈME ÉTAT; GIRL, PRONE; and one of the ISLAND DANCERS

ACTOR 4 plays TEACHER; MAN; DR. DAWKINS; Henri MATISSE; Abraham LINCOLN; Franklin Delano ROOSEVELT; BAS-RELIEF; STATE FAIR HEAD; GALLERIST; Dr. William McLELLAND; J. SINNOCK; MORTICIAN; VENDOR; DIME; J. Edgar HOOVER; AUCTIONEER; HERMAN Kobbe; and art pieces – all slides of work by eighteen European artists; MALE WHITE CLAY FIGURE; FISH; WHITE ANGEL; "NON JAMAIS" statue; and PLASTER OF PARIS LEG

SETTING

Settings are very fluid and seamlessly meld together. Blackouts are to be avoided. The play takes place in various locations:

- Selma's studio apartment in Harlem, New York
- Sarah Lawrence College, Yonkers, New York
- St. Agnes Hospital Nursing School, Raleigh, North Carolina
- a college lecture hall
- the atelier of Matisse in Paris
- the Oval Office, the White House, Washington, DC
- R.S. Lewis & Sons Funeral Home, Memphis, Tennessee
- a street corner in Harlem
- inside Selma's mind – a brass rectangle frame and a silver circle frame
- the office of John Sinnock, the United States Mint, Washington, DC
- the office of J. Edgar Hoover, FBI field office, New York, NY
- a New York City rooftop
- an auction house
- Selma Burke School of Sculpture, New York
- Marshall Park, Charlotte, North Carolina

TIME

The time is fluid and spans from 1925 to 1980.

PRODUCTION NOTES

NOTES ON THE TEXT

This play is a flight of fancy based on the incredible life and talent of Dr. Selma Hortense Burke. While many of the events in the play are based on true life, liberties have been taken. This isn't a biography, it isn't a fantasy, it's a drama with comic relief, and it isn't linear. It was written not to educate or to lecture but to entertain. Selma ages from age twenty to age ninety. She lived from 1900 to 1995, which is approximately 49,932,000 minutes – here, imagined, are ninety of them.

- / a slash indicates overlap of dialogue
- ... an ellipse at the end of a line indicates a self-censored thought or a trailing off
- – a dash indicates a cut-off or interruption

NOTES ON THE SET

The set may be lavish or minimal. A minimal set should at least have:

- a divan on wheels that can serve as the hospital bed and coffin
- a large box which becomes a desk or table or plinth (with three holes on one side so that heads may pop up)
- two easels
- a desk and chair
- a wheelchair
- a brass rectangle frame and a silver circular frame

Curtains on rod and pipe can be wheeled in or dropped in to confer and delineate space.

The representation of the art is more important than the set.

NOTES ON THE ART

The actors portray *all the art*. Actors' heads pop out of boxes to form busts; they could lie down on a skateboard to be pushed across the stage (as with the fish). They can be made bigger or smaller with shadows and light. Sometimes they step out of their surroundings as if being chiselled. Sometimes they are rigid and sometimes they are pliable. All but Lincoln and Lady Liberty are made, moulded, carved, and sculpted by Selma.

Directors and movement specialists may come together to interweave more than one body to make an image. The statues are always alive in Selma's mind, and they may have responses to her in the scenes. Sometimes they talk to her, argue, and sometimes they are a *comic counterpoint* to the seriousness of the scenes. They do not have agency.

The playwrights strongly encourage anyone producing the play to carry out extensive research on the art pieces and to use them to inspire and assist their production.

PRODUCTION STILLS

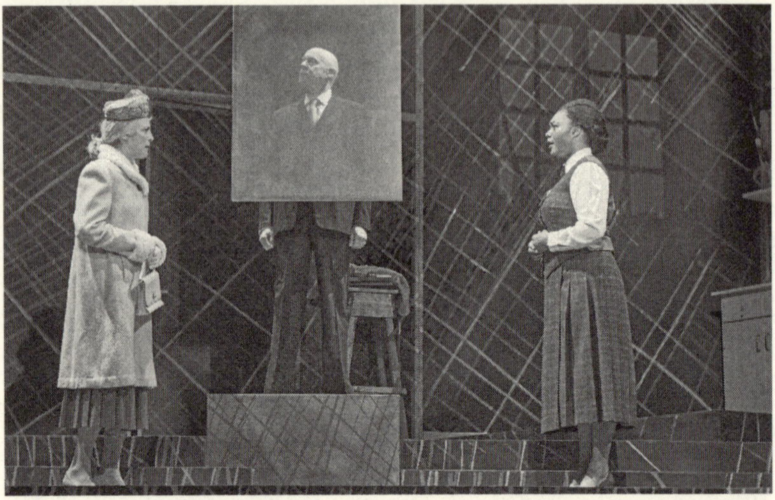

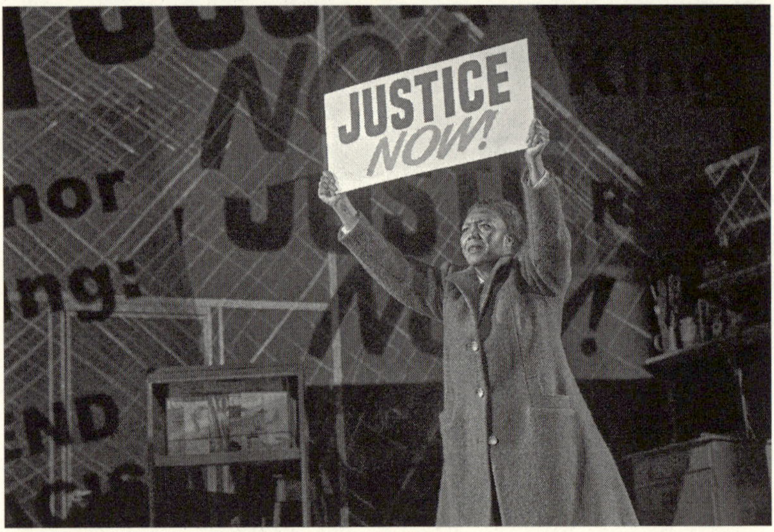

[TOP] Heather Pattengale, Christopher Hunt, and Norma Lewis in *Selma Burke*, April 2024; set design by Hanne Loosen, costume design by Adejoké Taiwo, lighting design by Tim Rodrigues, photo by Trudie Lee reproduced with permission

[BOTTOM] Norma Lewis in *Selma Burke*, April 2024; set design by Hanne Loosen, costume design by Adejoké Taiwo, lighting design by Tim Rodrigues, photo by Trudie Lee reproduced with permission

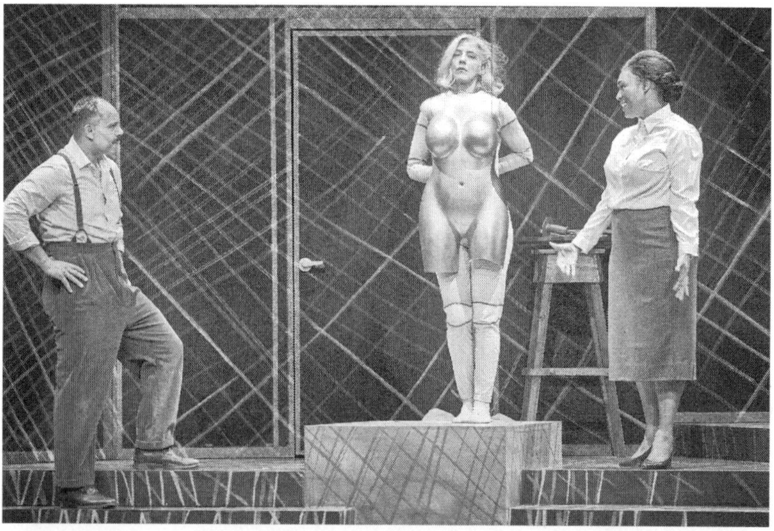

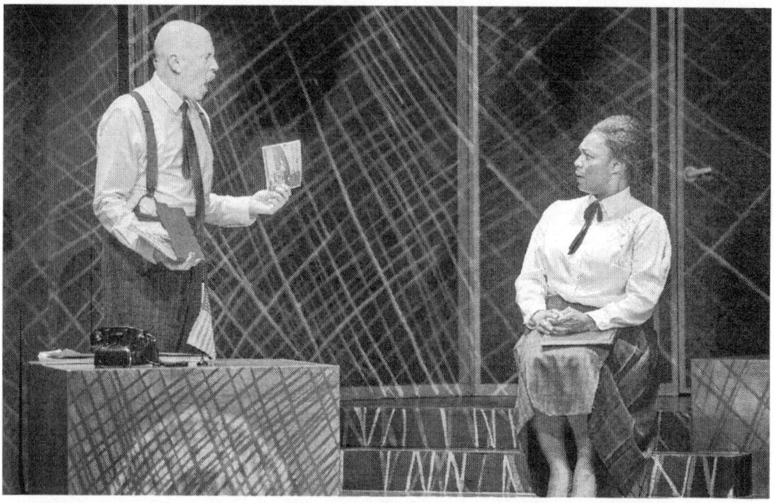

[TOP] Christopher Clare, Heather Pattengale, and Norma Lewis in *Selma Burke*, April 2024; set design by Hanne Loosen, costume design by Adejoké Taiwo, lighting design by Tim Rodrigues, photo by Trudie Lee reproduced with permission

[BOTTOM] Christopher Hunt and Norma Lewis in *Selma Burke*, April 2024; set design by Hanne Loosen, costume design by Adejoké Taiwo, lighting design by Tim Rodrigues, photo by Trudie Lee reproduced with permission

SCENE 1

You Don't Make It Easy

We hear bubbling noises. Spotlight up on steam wafting gently from an oversized pot. Enter a care worker, PATSY. Lights up on Selma's kitchen.

PATSY
(*calling out*) Morning Miss Selma, it's Patsy, day shift. (*scolding*) Miss Selma!

SELMA
(*offstage*) I'm working in here, child, don't interrupt.

PATSY
Miss Selma, I thought you agreed to no more cookin'. It's dangerous for you to be liftin' pots of soup at eighty years old! You could scald yourself badly. It's my job to look after you, that's what I am trying to do (*under her breath*) and you don't make it easy. (*calling back out*) We agreed your carers would cook your meals.

SELMA
(*offstage*) I'm not cooking.

PATSY
You are cooking!

SELMA
(*offstage*) I am rendering!

PATSY
What?

SELMA

(*offstage*) It's just some bones, you boil 'em so that you can pick off the meat, to keep the bones.

PATSY

That's called cooking!

SELMA

(*offstage*) That's called art.

PATSY

Where did you get this from?

PATSY looks inside the pot dubiously and freezes.

That. Is a human foot!

SELMA

(*offstage*) No it isn't.

PATSY

I can see the toenails.

PATSY crosses to the door and looks offstage.

And what the hell are you doin' up there on that ladder?

Lights cross-fade.

SCENE 2

Defying Papa

The corridor outside the studio at Sarah Lawrence College, Yonkers, New York. SELMA enters barefoot, wearing a hospital housecoat. PAPA follows, stopping her with his voice.

PAPA
Selma. Hortense. Burke.

SELMA
Papa! What are you doing here?

PAPA
Your Mama tol' me what you're doin' ...

SELMA
Papa, I want to be an artist.

PAPA
You are already an artist. See, I have this little face you made of clay when you were a little girl. I keep it in my pocket always, it's my talisman.

SELMA
I want to go to art school. I want to learn and earn extra money. I'm going to work as an artist's model and –

PAPA
An artist's model? You pose naked?!

SELMA
Yes, but –

PAPA

"You shall not uncover the nakedness of a woman … it is depravity," Leviticus 18:17. You mad, child? Are you cavorting with Satan?

SELMA

It's like nursing. Have any nurses seen you naked?

PAPA

That's different.

SELMA

Just like you, I'm taking off my clothes for a reason.

PAPA

No. I don't want you bringing the devil into this family. You walk through that door, and you will never see me again.

SELMA makes a hard choice and walks through the door, and PAPA shuffles off, rejected.

SCENE 2A

Art Studio Seduction

A curtain is dropped in that separates the two areas in the studio. There are an easel and divan. HANNAH follows SELMA into the room.

HANNAH
I will be sketching you for the anatomy portion of my portfolio. Sarah Lawrence College models after the Oxford and Cambridge system of one-on-one student-faculty tutorials. My art teacher is working in the adjacent studio and will be supervising intermittently, checking up on us. I know this is your first time modelling, and I just want to say I don't mind if you pull your robe up when he is in the room.

SELMA
I'm fine.

HANNAH
Does your husband mind you modelling in the nude?

SELMA
I'm a widow.

HANNAH
Oh, I'm sorry. I know that this can be good work for the disadvantaged or unemployed.

SELMA
I'm neither.

HANNAH
Oh! Where do you work?

SELMA
The hospital.

HANNAH
That's a lot of floors to mop. (*cheerfully*) I expect you have well-defined muscle structure.

SELMA
I'm actually a sculptor, but nursing pays the bills. It also gives me the opportunity to study the human form. (*lightly, matter-of-fact*) As a nurse I see people in all their adversities: the young, old, strong, weak, huddled in pain, limping, oozing pus from all their orifices.

HANNAH winces.

SELMA
Bodies that are battered and bruised from whippings and knifings. Dead bodies, slashed, strangled, shot, lynched ... (*enjoying HANNAH's discomfort*) I have seen a foot severed by a hunter's trap, an arm snapped off by a streetcar, a leg chewed off by animals –

HANNAH
Could, could you ...

HANNAH looks as though she's going to be sick.

SELMA
(*smiling*) But today, I present my very healthy body for *your* art.

SELMA drops the robe.

How would you like me to pose?

HANNAH
Oh, the divan. However, however you'd like, Selma.

HANNAH adjusts her easel.

Great. I'm going to need more light. (*calling out*) Excuse me, may I adjust the curtain to get more daylight?

The TEACHER pulls back the curtain to reveal CLAUDE in a chair, also posing nude. The two artists say nothing as they observe and apply paint to canvas and charcoal to paper. SELMA slowly turns her head, looks over at the other model. Returns to her pose. CLAUDE leans slowly in such a way as to surreptitiously look at SELMA. The TEACHER coughs gently. CLAUDE returns to his pose. SELMA smiles. SELMA and CLAUDE in unison slowly move their heads to see each other. They make eye contact.

Time passes. The session comes to an end. HANNAH shows SELMA her work. SELMA indicates "it's okay." HANNAH, not happy with her response, picks up the easel and leaves. CLAUDE watches as SELMA puts on her robe and with a little hip sway leaves the studio.

TEACHER

Okay McKay, that will do for today.

CLAUDE

I would prefer to be paid in cash after each sitting.

TEACHER

I'm afraid the college cuts the cheques weekly. (*showing CLAUDE the canvas*) What do you think?

CLAUDE

(*joking*) Obviously it was a little cold in the room.

TEACHER

I didn't feel a chill.

CLAUDE

(*intently*) Maybe we could have a redo in a less classical pose, (*beat*) let's try a different position.

TEACHER

(*relenting to the seduction*) Well, it's after class hours, and all the students are back in the dorm ... maybe I could pay, out of pocket, for a private session ...

The TEACHER draws the curtain.

SCENE 3

Anticipation

Selma's studio apartment. An isolated light comes up on the statue of the MOTHER. She is facing upstage. She has the cover cloth and with her arm underneath it makes what could be a Klan hood. SELMA takes the Klan hood and makes the sheet into a child for the MOTHER to hold. Lights shift into Selma's apartment. Soft jazz comes up. SELMA uncovers the sculpture.

SELMA
I invited him over not ... no ...

The MOTHER opens one eye in a "sure you're not" expression.

I'm not going to sleep with him ... no, I'm not!

The MOTHER winks "uh-huh."

A knock at the door. SELMA covers the MOTHER with a cloth. She admits CLAUDE.

CLAUDE
Girls who get naked for money are either usually enslaved by dope or the rebellious daughters of preachers.

SELMA
(*laughing*) Well now, yes, my father *is* a preacher.

CLAUDE
I overheard you say that you are a widow. I'm sorry. How?

SELMA

He was a mortician and he accidentally injected himself with embalming fluid.

CLAUDE

(*beat*) Now *there's* a story.

SELMA

You ever had a "needlestick injury"?

CLAUDE

Jamaican rum is more my poison.

SELMA

Where do you live?

CLAUDE

I'm a poet and a novelist. My ol' lady kicked me out, didn't want me doing my "little scribbles," as she called 'em.

SELMA

She wanted you to get a job?

CLAUDE

You know the only jobs available for me? Doorman, street sweeper, shoeshine –

SELMA

And you're too proud for that. Do you have babes to feed?

CLAUDE

My daughter, Hope. (*beat*) You must have babies.

SELMA

(*not sadly*) If I could have, I would have by now.

CLAUDE

(*pointing to the MOTHER*) So this isn't of you? It's very ... maternal.

SELMA

No. This is the first piece I did in wood.

CLAUDE

It has a certain naïveté.

The MOTHER reacts as if insulted.

SELMA

Well, actually, the first piece I did was a snow woman –

Flashback. Lights change, childlike music starts, and snow begins to fall. The MOTHER steps off her pedestal and crosses downstage. SELMA mimes making her, in three moves, into a tall, proud, well-endowed SNOW WOMAN. The SNOW WOMAN is childishly happy with her big breasts.

– in riverbed clay. A big snow woman. Tall and proud an' naked.

But then a man came along with a walking stick.

A MAN enters and looks the statue up and down.

MAN

Child, is this yours?

SELMA

(*proudly*) Yes, sir.

MAN

This isn't decent.

SELMA

Snow women don't have clothes except for a scarf and a hat.

MAN

We can't have that being seen by everyone walking along the river path!

SELMA
Statues are for everyone.

MAN
Who do you think you are?

SELMA
Selma Burke!

MAN
Then you better go ask your mother for a dress to put on this thing.

SELMA
Statues don't wear clothes. It's not a doll.

MAN
Don't you talk back to me.

SELMA
I was just explaining, because you don't seem to understand.

MAN
You are insolent and insubordinate, young lady. I'm going to teach you a lesson in morality.

The MAN comes at SELMA with his walking stick, and she ducks, afraid, but his target is the SNOW WOMAN, and he beats it into the ground. The SNOW WOMAN is decimated. SELMA is distraught. Lights change. SELMA covers the SNOW WOMAN up with the cloth.

SELMA
(*recovering from the memory, changing the subject*) So, are you published?

CLAUDE
My novel and my poetry.

SELMA

Oh yeah?

CLAUDE

The pages of my books are smuggled into prison and passed around like highly valued contraband.

SELMA

Does it inspire them?

CLAUDE

“If we must die, let it not be like hogs
Hunted and penned in an inglorious spot,
While round us bark the mad and hungry dogs,
Making their mock at our accursèd lot.
If we must die, O let us nobly die.
So that our precious blood may not be shed
In vain; then even the monsters we defy
Shall be constrained to honour us though dead!”

SELMA is impressed and decides to show him her best work.

CLAUDE

Well now, what’s under this one?

SELMA unveils it and turns it around. The actor who was the MOTHER now has no baby and has become LIGHT AND SHADOW, wearing a gold body shield on her torso. In black light her face, arms, and legs disappear and the gold shines.

SELMA

It’s my first expensive piece, a solid brass torso. It shines like gold. It’s called *Light and Shadow.*

CLAUDE

Well now, who was your model for this?

SELMA

I could barely afford the materials, I didn't have a model. I had a mirror.

SELMA adopts the same pose as LIGHT AND SHADOW.

CLAUDE

May I touch it?

SELMA

I believe that part of the beauty of sculpture is its tactile interaction.

CLAUDE

(*touching the neck with his fingers*) It's cool and smooth. (*moving to the shoulders*) Very nice.

SELMA

Why, thank you.

CLAUDE

(*tracing the side of the waist, the thigh, the leg, back up to the stomach, then to the breast*) She feels fine.

SELMA

Yes.

Their eyes lock as he slips his finger down and traces a triangle between LIGHT AND SHADOW's legs.

CLAUDE

I used to work in a kitchen, and working with all the hot pans left my fingertips dulled to the senses.

SELMA

What part of your body would be more sensitive?

CLAUDE

The fullness of my lips.

CLAUDE gently kisses LIGHT AND SHADOW's neck. He locks eyes with SELMA.

(*bantering*) This is just a factual assessment ...

CLAUDE kisses LIGHT AND SHADOW again.

SELMA
(*joining the banter*) So you can fully understand the materials ...

CLAUDE
Just for research.

CLAUDE kisses LIGHT AND SHADOW again.

SELMA
In order to have a fully immersive experience with the work.

CLAUDE
One must fully engage with art.

CLAUDE kisses the breast of LIGHT AND SHADOW, who remains neutral. SELMA, however, reacts with a slight intake of breath, almost inadvertently arching her back. CLAUDE drops to his knees in front of LIGHT AND SHADOW. As he kisses LIGHT AND SHADOW, SELMA's body reacts.

Lights change.

SCENE 4

The Decision

A room in a teaching hospital. The divan becomes a hospital bed. MRS. RIVERS is sitting in bed maniacally rocking back and forth, clutching a bundle wrapped in a blanket. SELMA stands beside her. DR. DAWKINS is holding a clipboard.

DR. DAWKINS

No other nurse has been able to help Mrs. Rivers. We don't want to use force. You're up.

SELMA

Yes, Doctor Dawkins.

SELMA turns to MRS. RIVERS.

Mrs. Rivers?

No reply.

Mrs. Rivers.

No reply.

I know you are hurting badly. I am not a mother, but I understand a little of what you are feeling, my heart aches for you. I am so sorry, so very sorry, but I have to take the baby away now. We have to examine her.

MRS. RIVERS

She was stillborn. What is wrong with you?

SELMA

We have procedures to follow. Mrs. Rivers, now she looks like a little baby girl, but rigor will set in, she will start to change, her little hands will become claws, her little cheeks will sink. You don't want to remember her like that.

MRS. RIVERS

I just want time to freeze this moment, this moment where she looks so perfect.

SELMA

(*seeing the doctor's clipboard*) I can do that for you.

SELMA takes the chart from DR. DAWKINS, flips the page over to the back of the chart, and takes the pen from his hand.

DR. DAWKINS

What are you doing?

SELMA

(*to MRS. RIVERS*) Hold still.

MRS. RIVERS stops rocking. She holds the pose as SELMA draws. SELMA holds out the sketch for MRS. RIVERS to see. MRS. RIVERS's face melts, and she starts to cry.

Pause.

MRS. RIVERS holds out the bundle. SELMA gives her the picture and takes the baby.

DR. DAWKINS

You'll need to take this down to the morgue.

SELMA

You take her to the morgue.

SELMA hands the baby to DR. DAWKINS.

DR. DAWKINS
And where are you going?

SELMA
Art school.

Lights cross-fade.

SCENE 5

Leaving the USA

*Art school. The large box, upright, is now a lectern. As the scene progresses, in a rectangle box of light, Actor 4 enacts the slides, adjusting his pose or facial expression as the list of artists is read out. The **PROFESSOR** stands at the lectern and clicks various slides to illustrate the artists in her lecture. We hear the familiar click of the carousel changing on the projector. **SELMA** sits in the chair looking up at her **PROFESSOR**.*

PROFESSOR

Welcome to art history. I have curated for you the art of the geniuses who invite us to see the world through their eyes. Botticelli. Michelangelo. Jan van Eyck. El Greco. Da Vinci. Raphael. Rembrandt. Caravaggio. Rubens. Constable. Turner. Rodin. Gaugin. Seurat. Degas.

Actor 4 as the "slide" covers his ear and looks deranged.

Van Gogh! Right up to the contemporary masterworks of Picasso and Matisse.

SELMA raises her hand.

PROFESSOR

Yes, Miss Burke.

SELMA

You know *my* name out of all the students here?

PROFESSOR

You're the only – one of the women.

SELMA
Are we only going to learn about European art?

PROFESSOR
I think I know what you are asking. An example would be Matisse. In 1906 he took a trip to North Africa and fell in love with an African statue. Matisse used this image throughout the course of his career. This was considered revolutionary.

SELMA
Isn't that considered theft?

PROFESSOR
Homage. (*to the class*) Matisse would see this as a form of cultural exchange –

SELMA
Where is Matisse?

PROFESSOR
He's in Paris. He works in his atelier, where he takes in a very select few *gifted* proteges.

SELMA
He'll take me.

SELMA gets up and leaves.

SCENE 6

The Oath

Matisse's atelier, Paris. MATISSE conducts the lesson while working on his sculpture, MATISSE RECLINING NUDE, illustrating technique as he instructs. SELMA follows along, mirroring him, working on her BURKE RECLINING NUDE. The sculptures are Actor 3, who adjusts her body to the left or right depending on who is sculpting her.

MATISSE
Let's continue with the lesson. What is art?

SELMA
Painting, writing, sculpture –

MATISSE
Art is an invitation. An invitation to a conversation. It says, "This is how I see the world. Do you like this lens? What do you see? Que voyez-vous? Do you want to have this conversation with me? Do you see the technique? Do you see the person behind the art?" Did you go to the Louvre?

SELMA
Everything is so grand in scale and composition. Which do you like?

MATISSE
Most of it is not to my taste. I'm just sorry there is so little for you to see.

SELMA
So little? I was overwhelmed by it all!

MATISSE
Well, modern art isn't there, and of the antiquities we lost so much.

SELMA
When?

MATISSE
We had this little thing called the French Revolution.

SELMA
The peasant uprising, the rebellion against the monarchy. They were justified. They were hungry.

MATISSE
But in their zeal to overthrow, they destroyed so many statues, so many frescos, so many oils.

SELMA
They felt justified, having been exploited.

MATISSE
The need to punish others is not a good motivation to deprive your children of the bounty of artists.

SELMA
Their children were deprived of food.

MATISSE
Selling art would buy bread, destroying it – no. Art should never be destroyed.

SELMA
What if it's just bad art?

SELMA steps back, looks at what she has been moulding, and beats it back down. BURKE RECLINING NUDE protests sadly as her nose hits the floor.

MATISSE
In whose eyes?

SELMA
Mine. I sometimes make bad art.

BURKE RECLINING NUDE becomes confident, sexy.

MATISSE
On the way to good art, and good art on the way to great art.

SELMA
Maybe.

MATISSE
Definitely. One, you will always have a reference point for how far you've come, and two, your worst might be seen as someone's preference. No. You should never destroy art.

BURKE RECLINING NUDE switches, and SELMA begins to remodel her.

SELMA
Critics destroy art.

MATISSE
Only metaphorically. The poor are angry that money was spent on art, so they destroy it. The uneducated don't understand art, and so they destroy it. Parents destroy it because they want to protect les enfants. Les politiciens think it is propaganda for the other side, and so they destroy it. The military destroy it because it has no worth in battle. The religious destroy it because it is idolatrous or wicked. The chaste destroy it because they think is so powerful it will incite them to lust and all the pleasures they deny themselves. Everyone has a good reason to rip it down.

SELMA
Not me.

MATISSE

Yes, even you.

SELMA

No.

MATISSE

There will come a time when you are asked to destroy art for a good cause, for a right cause, for a noble cause, but no matter the subject, no matter the slight, you must not.

MATISSE holds up his hand as if swearing on a bible.

Never. Jamais.

SELMA

(*copying him, swearing her oath*) Non. Jamais.

Pause.

MATISSE

Let me see your work.

MATISSE goes over to her BURKE RECLINING NUDE. He looks. SELMA holds her breath.

MATISSE

This will not do.

SELMA

Monsieur Matisse, it is almost *exactly* as yours is.

MATISSE

C'est un problème.

SELMA

What's the problem?

MATISSE

You are not here to make the art of Henri Matisse, you are here to make the art of Selma Burke.

SELMA

Ah, but I *can* make the same art as Matisse.

SELMA smiles with satisfaction.

MATISSE

Oui.

SCENE 7

Claude Breaks the Intimacy

Selma's studio apartment. SELMA is working on FEMALE WHITE CLAY FIGURE and MALE WHITE CLAY FIGURE. With a wooden-handled clay loop, she smooths the woman's cheek and then the man's nose. They are facing each other; it is obviously intimate; they may be about to kiss. CLAUDE is drinking rum, staring moodily out the window.

SELMA

Claude, c'est bon, n'est-ce pas? You've seen more art in Europe than I have, what do you think?

CLAUDE looks at FEMALE WHITE CLAY FIGURE and MALE WHITE CLAY FIGURE, breaking the intimate connection between them.

CLAUDE

Sentimental benign crap.

CLAUDE takes his thumb and smushes it into the wet clay, creasing MALE WHITE CLAY FIGURE's eye to an ugly wink and curling FEMALE WHITE CLAY FIGURE's mouth cruelly.

SELMA

Claude!

CLAUDE

This work is derivative. You need to think like a modern Negro. It's good, but it can be outstanding. You, me, we are the New Negros, we must embrace it.

SELMA

If you've become the New Negro since I've been gone, I want the old one back.

CLAUDE

If I'm not wanted around here, I'll leave.

SELMA

Yes go, go sleep at Langston's. You think I don't know what's going on? Try tearing up some of his poems. See how he likes it.

CLAUDE stops at the door, then takes a letter out of his pocket.

CLAUDE

I can't get a commission, an agent, or a publisher, and you –

SELMA

Me what?

CLAUDE

You know that contest you entered before you went away –

SELMA

I never heard –

CLAUDE hands her the letter.

CLAUDE

I can't catch a single break. You ... you are going to the White House.

SELMA

Why did you open ... Jesus! Claude, when did this arrive? *When were you going to give this to me*?

CLAUDE

I just did.

SELMA

I have to be *in Washington tomorrow*!

CLAUDE

(*flatly*) Congratulations.

SCENE 8

Selma Goes to the White House

Outside the Oval Office. SELMA rushes in and a SECRETARY looks down at her clipboard disapprovingly.

SELMA
Selma Burke. I'm here to see the president.

SECRETARY
Have a seat. The chair next to the bust.

The SECRETARY exits. LINCOLN's head pops through the plinth.

SELMA
Oh, Lincoln. Hey.

LINCOLN
You're late to meet the sitting president of the United States of America with sweaty underarms? Carrying –

SELMA
The art store was closed. It's butcher's paper.

LINCOLN
Very professional –

SELMA
It took five hours to drive here. I had to promise the cabby I'd do sketches of his whole family. The guy has forty-seven kids!

LINCOLN
You're late, you screwed up.

SELMA

You screwed up, too, you didn't give us any property rights for those cotton fields ...

LINCOLN's head disappears. The SECRETARY comes back and motions SELMA into the office.

SECRETARY

You're late!

SELMA

I'm so sorry, my husband, never mind ... I'm sorry.

Franklin Delano ROOSEVELT is in a wheelchair.

ROOSEVELT

Hello, Miss Burke. Welcome.

SELMA

Mr. President, thank you so much for granting me the time to meet with you.

ROOSEVELT

Not at all, Miss Burke, it's a wonderful excuse to get away from all the affairs of state.

SELMA

Thank you, sir. The light is better by the window.

ROOSEVELT

I prefer to sit behind my desk.

SELMA

It's just your face, Mr. President, no one is going to see – the desk.

ROOSEVELT

Fine.

ROOSEVELT wheels himself over to the window, catching the wheelchair on something.

SELMA
Would you like a hand?

ROOSEVELT looks at her.

SELMA
Sorry, I know you're very capable.

ROOSEVELT angles his chair.

SELMA
Can you please turn your head and look right for me, sir?

ROOSEVELT
Where are you from?

SELMA
New York City.

ROOSEVELT
I like New York. A lot of Democrats there.

SELMA
Please, if you could just sit still –

ROOSEVELT
You've received several fellowships.

SELMA
Yes.

ROOSEVELT
And the selection committee was impressed that you studied in Paris under Matisse.

SELMA
I was able to teach him a few things.

ROOSEVELT laughs.

SELMA
Please! Hold the pose!

ROOSEVELT
You got out of Europe before that madman began his rampage. Have you been doing your part for the war effort here at home?

SELMA
I drove a truck for the Brooklyn navy yard, but I injured my back.

ROOSEVELT
Lucky to get better. With polio, no damn cure.

SELMA
Surely scientists are –

ROOSEVELT
Always tell me they need more money for research!

SELMA
Can't the government fund it?

ROOSEVELT
If I gave extra money for something that the Republicans say I have a vested interest in, they'd roast me alive.

SELMA
Republicans don't get polio?

ROOSEVELT
You're right it's a bipartisan issue.

SELMA
Make it a charity. I'm sure if every American paid just one dime, that would add up to a lot of dimes for research and a cure –

ROOSEVELT
The treasury could even reissue the dime with my face on it. That would really irk the Republicans.

SELMA and ROOSEVELT laugh.

ROOSEVELT
We would need a slogan: "Dimes, so that children can walk." "The walk of dimes"?

SELMA
"The march of polio?" (*hearing herself*) No!

ROOSEVELT
"The march of dimes?"

At this point, SELMA walks up to ROOSEVELT and holds his head in both hands. Chagrined, he holds still.

Lights change.

SCENE 9

The Bas-Relief Meets Eleanor Roosevelt

Selma's studio apartment. A brass frame is dropped in. ROOSEVELT, as a bronze plaque, faces SELMA, who fidgets with a cloth.

SELMA
The commission states that if Eleanor Roosevelt doesn't approve of you, there will be no unveiling. I don't know if she's going to like you.

ROOSEVELT
She isn't, she doesn't want to see *my* face. When I died, she found out about my affair.

SELMA
I'm bringing her face-to-face with you for the first time since she found out you were a big ol' cheat.

ROOSEVELT
She's going to want to see a shrivelled up, worn-out man, and you made me look younger and handsome.

SELMA
She's not going to be happy, maybe I should redesign you with an arrow through your head –

ROOSEVELT
– And you're making her come to Harlem, she's going to be all nervous about that, she'll probably bring her chauffeur up with her for protection.

We hear a knock on the front door. SELMA covers ROOSEVELT up. SELMA opens the door to ELEANOR. Her CHAUFFEUR is behind her.

SELMA
Good morning. Mrs. Roosevelt. Welcome.

ELEANOR enters with her CHAUFFEUR.

ELEANOR
(*a little nervously*) Good morning, Mrs. Burke.

ELEANOR and SELMA shake hands.

ELEANOR
We can't stay long. I've got a ribbon cutting, and we're running behind schedule. Is the plaque ready to view?

SELMA removes the cloth and steps back.

ELEANOR
(*disapprovingly*) Oh ...

ROOSEVELT
Hi honey, what do you think of your ol' man?

ELEANOR
When he sat for you, how old did you think he was?

SELMA
Sixty-two.

ELEANOR
He was ailing.

SELMA
I am aware of that. He was so gracious.

ELEANOR

But here you have made him seem like a youthful, vigorous man.

ROOSEVELT

Told ya.

ELEANOR

Could you not see what he looked like by then?

SELMA

Yes.

ELEANOR

Then why on earth would you depict him as if he were a young, healthy man?

ROOSEVELT responds proudly.

SELMA

I did see that he looked ... reduced.

ROOSEVELT

Reduced?

ELEANOR

He was in pain every day of his life. He survived four gruelling campaigns. He suffered the loss of fellow Americans *he* sent to fight and die. Where is *that etched on his face*?

SELMA

I have not done this image for today, but for tomorrow and tomorrow. Five hundred years from now, America and all the world will want to look on our president, not as he was the last few months before he died, but as we saw him for most of the time he was with us – strong, so full of life, and with that wonderful look of going forward.

ROOSEVELT
Atta girl.

ELEANOR
(*making a decision*) Well, until the unveiling.

ELEANOR exits. The CHAUFFEUR gives her a thumbs up as they exit together.

CHAUFFEUR
At least there's going to be an unveiling.

SELMA appreciates the comment and looks to ROOSEVELT, who wipes his forehead, signalling "that was close."

The lights transition.

SCENE 9A

The Unveiling in Washington

SELMA unveils the Roosevelt BAS-RELIEF. We hear the sound of applause, cameras pop, and band music plays. SELMA bows.

Lights change, and a hurried ticking speeds up as the next scene progresses.

SCENE 10

The Game of Rejection

ALL are on stage and switch positions rapidly. We hear the sound of knocking. The TURKEY is crouched on the pedestal, hands under armpits for wings, head on one side. Its tongue comically protrudes. The STATE FAIR HEAD stands beside it.

SELMA
You are the head of the committee for the state fair?

STATE FAIR HEAD
Yes.

SELMA
I've made this maquette of a turkey. If you like it, I will make more and set up a booth to sell them.

TURKEY
(*proudly*) Gobble, gobble.

STATE FAIR HEAD
No. My sister-in-law has the Thanksgiving decorations – this will be a competition. Make something not Thanksgiving related.

TURKEY
(*sadly*) Gobble gobble.

The TURKEY gets off the pedestal and is replaced by the FISH. We hear the sound of knocking and music underneath it that becomes increasingly frantic.

SELMA
You are the head of the committee for the exhibition?

EXPO HEAD
Yes.

SELMA
I've made this fish.

The FISH makes "bubble bop bop bop" noises proudly and demonstrates its fine fins.

EXPO HEAD
This is an exposition, not a state fair! Make something bigger, more serious.

FISH
(*sadly*) Bop bop bop.

The FISH on the pedestal turns around and SELMA makes a tall, proud WHITE ANGEL.

More knocking.

SELMA
You are the head of the gallery?

GALLERY HEAD
Yes.

SELMA
I've made this angel done in the style of Michelangelo!

GALLERY HEAD
This is a gallery for Black art, we don't want some white angel. Make something Afrocentric.

The WHITE ANGEL sadly droops its wings in disappointment, steps off the pedestal, and is replaced by an AFRICAN MASK figure who strikes a warrior pose.

More knocking.

SELMA
You are the head of the –

GALLERIST
No!

SELMA
It's an African mask –

GALLERIST
No!

The music ends with a "wah wah" sound. The AFRICAN MASK makes a kicking motion like a disappointed six-year-old boy being told he couldn't play baseball. The lights transition.

SCENE 11

I'm Not Going to Selma – Claude, I Am Selma

Selma's studio. A WHITE FACE pops up from her work bench.

SELMA

You are my last supply of plaster of paris – I'm going to have to go back to nursing –

WHITE FACE

You can't work on me now. The Selma to Montgomery march starts on Sunday. It's got your name, it's like a sign from God. Selma to Montgomery.

SELMA

You are the only commission I've had in six months. I can't. I have to finish you.

The phone rings. SELMA answers.

Hello. (*beat*) This is she!

SELMA listens into the phone.

WHITE FACE

Who is it?

SELMA

(*thrilled*) Thank you, thank you. Yes, I can make that deadline, you can count on me. (*hanging up*) It's the Performing Arts Center in Milwaukee! I just got a big commission –

WHITE FACE

Claude will want you to go to the march. He's not going to like it –

CLAUDE bursts in excitedly.

CLAUDE

Selma, pack your bags, we're going. It's happening, baby, and we are going!

SELMA

You and who are going?

CLAUDE

Me, you, Selwyn and his brother, and some other friends of his. He is driving down, and he has space in his car for us.

CLAUDE crosses and exits.

(*offstage, calling out*) He wants to get on the road early, so we have to be ready by six tomorrow morning.

WHITE FACE

I told you so.

SELMA

I don't remember being consulted on this.

CLAUDE

(*offstage, calling out*) There are going to be thousands –

CLAUDE reappears with a suitcase.

SELMA

I can't, Claude.

CLAUDE

What do you mean, you can't? It's your duty. It's all our duty.

SELMA
It's fifty-four miles walking for five days straight. I ain't got that kind o' time.

CLAUDE
What are you doin' that's mo' important than civil rights? Voter registration? You're aware of what's going on down south, ain't you? The state troopers brutally attacked *six hundred* on the Edmund Pettus Bridge.

SELMA
There's going to be trouble again, you know that –

CLAUDE
Doctor King says it will be a nonviolent march.

SELMA
Claude, it doesn't matter what Reverend King says. It ain't up to us. Violence will be done no matter how nonviolent we want to be.

CLAUDE
They won't dare. Too many cameras will be there this time. The world will be watching. You're coming.

SELMA
(*excitedly sharing her news*) Baby, I just got a commission! Duke Ellington.

CLAUDE
You know your work ain't going to change shit.

SELMA is stung to her core.

CLAUDE
How is your work comparable to people who are putting their lives on the line to gain our rights, huh? You in your studio playing with clay instead of –

SELMA

I am not playing ... *You* are trying to trivialize my work again. I am immortalizing and celebrating the life of one of our heroes.

CLAUDE

You need to concentrate on the important things in life.

WHITE FACE

Me thinks you're jealous. That is so petty.

SELMA

Let me tell you, if I don't work, no bills get paid around here, the rent, food, heat, electricity. Nothing. I don't see you bringing in any money. Every job you're offered you think is beneath you. My work is important to me, and it should be to you too. You want me to tell those folks writing the cheque, "No. I can't make my deadline, because I'm going for a walk in Alabama?"

CLAUDE

Now who's trivializing? It's not a walk, and I'm not jealous of –

SELMA

Ellington is a genius. He's a composer who conducts from the piano bench. You know who were the geniuses doing that before? Haydn! Mozart! You think they don't have hundreds of busts of their faces in concert halls, opera houses, museums, and in the parlours of rich white people's houses? Who's immortalizing our people?

CLAUDE

And who's celebrating my contribution?

WHITE FACE

Oh, for Christ's sake, why are we talking about him now?

Softening, SELMA goes to CLAUDE.

SELMA
I have sketched you dozens of times, it's what my hand naturally does. I drew you at breakfast last week on a napkin –

CLAUDE breaks away from SELMA.

CLAUDE
I am a napkin. A napkin you are going to throw in the garbage after you have wiped your mouth with me.

SELMA
(*trying again*) I thought you had modelled so many times, it was work. I didn't want you to work for me. That's why I capture you when you're still, doing other things, reading the paper at the breakfast table, writing on the fire escape –

CLAUDE
But no bust of me. No sculpture of me!

SELMA
I didn't think –

CLAUDE
It's time to put down your chisel and hammer and pick up a placard.

WHITE FACE
No.

CLAUDE
Sel, go pack a case for the trip.

SELMA
Don't tell me what to do.

CLAUDE
Go. Pack. Your. Case.

CLAUDE crosses to SELMA menacingly.

SELMA
Leave me alone!

They hold a moment. CLAUDE storms out with his suitcase. SELMA picks up a hammer and chisel and moves towards WHITE FACE.

WHITE FACE
Hey! Be careful with that. Don't take my nose off!

SELMA
It's okay, baby.

WHITE FACE
I trust you.

SELMA resumes her work. Lights change.

SCENE 12

The Trouble with Triples

Selma's studio apartment. SELMA turns to three blobs of clay waiting to be worked on. Each turns around as SELMA sculpts them. As each character speaks, SELMA turns from one to the other to sculpt them. Jazz plays. A clay head pops up. It is DUKE Ellington.

DUKE
You are a mighty fine woman, Miss Selma. Your husband is a lucky man. I myself likes a woman who's built sturdy like you.

SELMA
Who you calling sturdy?

DUKE
Ain't nothin' wrong with sturdy, Miss Selma. You know we Black men like our women with some meat on them. When you make love to a woman, you want to feel somethin' in your arms, not a scarecrow with a dress on.

SELMA
Look, Mr. Ellington –

DUKE
Duke –

SELMA
I ain't got time for flirtin'.

DUKE
I ain't stopping you from doing your job.

SELMA

How'd you like it if I came flirtin' around you while you rehearsin' or composin'?

DUKE

I would say, "Bring it on, sistah."

SELMA gives him a look. The jazz is replaced by soulful klezmer. A woman's head, KELLER, pops up and looks anxiously over her shoulder at DUKE. He doesn't freeze but looks on.

KELLER

I'm here for you to model.

SELMA

I'm so glad that you made it out of Germany.

KELLER

(*matter of fact, not melodramatically*) My husband was burned alive along with the family that hid us. I escaped with our daughter.

SELMA

I'm glad you both escaped –

KELLER

– she got a gash in her foot, it got infected. Just after we crossed the French border, she died.

SELMA

I'll make sure your face tells your story.

The klezmer is replaced by white Christian music. A third head, McLELLAND, pops up.

McLELLAND

Make me look handsome.

SELMA
I'll do my best.

McLELLAND
I realize this isn't exactly a labour of love for you, is it?

SELMA
I made a deal with the head librarian. I will donate this bust of you to the library, and they will change the policy to allow little Black children to borrow books.

McLELLAND
You're working for free?

SELMA
Yes, you have to make a deal with the devil sometimes.

DUKE
Why you spending your time with these whiteys? You should be concentrating on your own people.

KELLER
She is sculpting me because she wants to make everyone aware of the horrors of fascism.

McLELLAND
She wants Black children getting access to books, so that they too can succeed.

DUKE
I'm celebrating excellence.

KELLER
I'm drawing attention to the atrocities of the nazis.

McLELLAND
I'm the saintly Christian opening doors.

DUKE
I am the pinnacle of success!

KELLER
I am the warning that can't be ignored.

McLELLAND
I am the conduit to change.

DUKE
I'm the Harlem Renaissance –

KELLER
I'm the persecuted Jew –

McLELLAND
I'm access to knowledge –

DUKE
/I'm addressing imbalance in recognition.

KELLER
/I'm the candle in the darkness.

McLELLAND
/I'm the practical solution.

DUKE and KELLER and McLELLAND
Spend more time with me!

Like petulant children, DUKE, KELLER, and McLELLAND get louder as they sing.

DUKE
/(*singing*) It don't mean a thing, if it ain't got that swing, doo wop, doo wop.

KELLER
/(*singing*) Baruch atah Adonai Eloheinu melech ha-olam.

McLELLAND

/(*singing*) Oh when the saints go marching in, oh when the saints go marching in.

SELMA stops them, exhausted. Lights shift.

SCENE 13

The Bugging of Washington

Split stage, Selma's studio and Sinnock's office. Lights up in the office, where MARSHA picks up the phone and lays the receiver on the desk. She holds a tube with sketches in it. SELMA is in her studio working on the GENTLEMAN sculpture, tool in one hand and phone in the other.

GENTLEMAN
You've become a spy!

SELMA
(*to the GENTLEMAN*) I'm about to listen in on a conversation. Sounds like some bigwig up in Washington wants to look at my old sketches of FDR.

GENTLEMAN
Maybe they want to exhibit them now that the president has died.

SELMA shrugs. SINNOCK enters and MARSHA masks the phone so that he can't see it.

SINNOCK
Thanks, Marsha.

SINNOCK takes the sketches out of the tube.

I appreciate you letting me have these. I will get them back to you in a few days.

MARSHA
What's this all about? All the secrecy and cloak-and-dagger stuff. Anyone would think you are after state secrets. (*goading him*) I don't think her designs are all that good.

SINNOCK
That's where you're wrong, Marsha, her work is extraordinary.

GENTLEMAN
(*to SELMA*) You are extraordinary!

MARSHA
Why do you need to take the sketches with you?

SINNOCK
The director herself chose me to do FDR's portrait –

MARSHA
Oh sure, because he created the March of Dimes, they want to commemorate him by putting him –

SINNOCK
– on the dime.

MARSHA
They want to mark his birthday when everyone is still feeling the loss.

SINNOCK
This puts me under a lot of pressure.

SELMA
(*to the GENTLEMAN*) That's not enough time.

MARSHA angles the phone so that SELMA can hear clearly.

MARSHA
So why do you need Burke's drawings?

SINNOCK
It doesn't mean I'm copying it.

MARSHA
/Uh-huh.

GENTLEMAN
/Sure!

MARSHA
You asked me to meet you after hours and not to tell anyone.

SINNOCK
I just didn't want people getting involved in my concerns. Washingtonians are such gossips. And there are rumours that government offices are being bugged!

MARSHA surreptitiously hangs up the phone. As does SELMA. SELMA smiles at the GENTLEMAN.

SCENE 13A

Stolen Art

The BAS-RELIEF changes from the profile of Roosevelt and now has the words "LIBERTY" and "IN GOD WE TRUST" and the initials "J.S." on it.

SCENE 14

Smashed Art

Selma's studio apartment. SELMA is working on a sculpture of an ABSTRACT NUDE. CLAUDE enters.

SELMA
Claude, welcome home, I saw some of the march on the news!

SELMA and CLAUDE hug.

CLAUDE
You should have been there.

SELMA
I've been working like crazy ... I'm tired. I need to sit down.

CLAUDE
You're tired?

CLAUDE shows her the soles of his shoes to demonstrate how worn they are. SELMA sits, and CLAUDE kneels before her.

SELMA
What are you doing? If you are going to ask me to remarry you again, you can forget it.

CLAUDE
Come with me to Memphis –

SELMA
You just got home. Memphis?!

CLAUDE

To support the sanitation workers in their strike. Rev. King will be there tomorrow night to address the workers. Come with me.

SELMA

Claude –

CLAUDE

It's not a march this time, you won't have to be on your feet for too long. The working conditions of the sanitation workers get worse every day. They're getting killed, crushed by old malfunctioning equipment, and the mayor and the city turn a blind eye. I've been working on this –

CLAUDE pulls out his notebook.

I call it "Workers of the World Unite."

SELMA

That's great, Claude, but you can take your notebook on the road. I need my studio. My work –

CLAUDE

(*mimicking her*) "My work." You hide behind your work to do nothing.

SELMA

If I don't work –

CLAUDE

I'm sick and tired of you standing by the sidelines –

SELMA

If *you* have to go back – go –

CLAUDE

Our people are dying, and all you do is whittle wood! What's the use of immortalizing some people while others are being gunned down on the street?!

Picking up her mallet, CLAUDE goes over to her ABSTRACT NUDE and in three strikes smashes it to the ground. SELMA is on her knees.

SELMA

Claude, go to Memphis and Don't. Come. Back.

CLAUDE storms out. SELMA goes to the collapsed ABSTRACT NUDE, and they hug. SELMA helps the ABSTRACT NUDE up from the ground. SELMA fashions her arm into a Black power salute as the lights shift into a split scene.

SCENE 14A

Murder

We see Dr. KING in a spotlight "addressing" the crowd, as we hear:

KING

(*voiceover*) Somewhere I read of the freedom of assembly. Somewhere I read of the freedom of speech. Somewhere I read of the freedom of the press. Somewhere I read that the greatness of America is the right to protest for right.

A deafening rifle shot rings out. SELMA, ABSTRACT NUDE, and KING all respond as if shot. The sound reverberates throughout the theatre. Lights down on the studio. KING is in slow motion, responding to the trajectory of the shot, bathed in gold light.

SCENE 14B

Despair

Lights cross-fade to the apartment, where SELMA mimics DESPAIR.

SELMA slowly stands, wiping tears as the faint strains of organ music are heard.

DESPAIR
You're leaving me?

SELMA
I'm going to the funeral.

DESPAIR
You'll miss your client's deadline.

SELMA
Yes.

SCENE 15

Reconstruction

Dr. KING lies in state at the R.S. Lewis & Sons Funeral Home, Memphis. Organ music grows louder. The divan becomes a coffin. SELMA stands over the body of Dr. KING studying his face, then crosses to the MORTICIAN standing nearby. He is a man used to working with emotional women; he is patient and understanding.

MORTICIAN
I'm so sorry for your loss. For our loss.

SELMA
I understand you are the person who prepared Doctor King for the viewing.

MORTICIAN
(*cautiously*) I did.

SELMA
You would have done the jaw reconstruction with mortuary wax. You got his jaw line *almost* perfect.

MORTICIAN
(*trying not to feel slighted*) You're a mortician?

SELMA
I'm a sculptor.

MORTICIAN
I see.

SELMA
The material you used for the jaw reconstruction, it's red.

MORTICIAN
Yes.

SELMA
It's showing.

MORTICIAN
I did the best I could.

SELMA
Then please adjust the colour of the face to cover the reconstruction.

MORTICIAN
People keep touching his face –

SELMA
It's not hard to fix.

MORTICIAN
Madam, the viewing is in progress, we have lines around the block. I can't hold up the proceedings.

SELMA
It would be a quick fix.

MORTICIAN
My work on Doctor King has concluded. It's over.

Pause. Stalemate. Then SELMA opens her purse and takes out some makeup.

SELMA
I'll fix this.

SELMA goes to apply the makeup to Dr. KING's face.

We shall overcome.

SCENE 16

The Art Gives Advice

Lights up on the studio apartment. SELMA is working on a sculpture of a PROTESTER, who seems to carry an invisible sign.

PROTESTER
You have to finish me!

SELMA
But they *assassinated* him ...

PROTESTER
But the riots, you won't be safe –

SELMA
Well ...

PROTESTER
Do you want to disappoint another client? –

SELMA
– And disappoint my people?

PROTESTER
There will always be something to march for. And the violence! Claude got his wrist broken. How are you going to finish me with a broken wrist?

SELMA stands back and looks at the PROTESTER.

SELMA
Something's not quite right ... Maybe you need something to hold.

SELMA places a sign in the PROTESTER's arms. The PROTESTER steps off the pedestal and hands the sign back to SELMA.

PROTESTER
(*beat*) It's time for you to hold it.

SELMA turns the sign around. It says "Justice Now." Scared and looking around, she holds it above her head, marching defiantly. We hear sounds of chanting and marching, which cross-fade to traffic noises.

SCENE 17

That's My Face!

New York street. A VENDOR with a stack of newspapers.

VENDOR
Paper! Get your evening paper ...

SELMA
(*running over to him*) Yes! My friend told me that she saw my photo in the paper. In the march!

VENDOR
(*uninterested*) Uh-huh. Fifteen cents.

SELMA hands him a quarter and sees her picture.

SELMA
Yep! Here I am!

VENDOR
Uh-huh. Here's your change.

SELMA looks at the dime. She is stunned.

SELMA
That's my face.

VENDOR
(*looks over*) Nuh-uh. That's FDR.

SELMA
I did that.

VENDOR

(*implying "Sure you did, lady"*) Uh-huh. You don't want it, you could always give it to me as a tip.

SELMA forages around in her pocket and gives the VENDOR a dollar. Her fingers curl around the dime, making a fist. Then she opens her fist and studies the engraving.

SELMA

J.S.

SCENE 18

The Mental Battle

Actor 4 holds up two frames, one gold and one silver, and switches them between the profiles of BAS-RELIEF and DIME. SELMA sits with her back to them.

BAS-RELIEF
FDR. Thirty-second president of the United States. I'm brass.

DIME
FDR. Thirty-second president of the United States. I'm silver.

BAS-RELIEF
People come to admire me all the time in this elegant building.

DIME
There is one of you and millions of me. I was designed by the chief engraver of the mint himself, John Sinnock –

BAS-RELIEF
Except you weren't. *He copied her sketches.*

DIME
He didn't.

BAS-RELIEF
Did. *Same* profile, *same* angle, *same* hollow of the cheek, *same* whorl on the ear, *same* slope of the nose –

DIME
You have one lock of hair that is slightly flatter.

BAS-RELIEF
Your forehead has one more wrinkle, but your provenance is me.

SELMA
(*to DIME*) Face it.

The frames overlap and freeze.

DIME
(*to SELMA*) Confront the bastard.

SELMA
I guess I'm going back to Washington.

SCENE 19

The Sin of Sinnock

The United States Mint office of John SINNOCK. SELMA enters. SINNOCK is startled, recognizing her right away but pretending he doesn't.

SELMA
Selma Burke. Do you have anything you want to say to me, Mr. Sinnock?

SINNOCK
How did you get into a secure building?

SELMA
I did the bas-relief, which you plagiarized for the dime.

SINNOCK
(*mansplaining*) As a *numismatic* sculptor, I reference many sources.

SELMA
It's *clearly* my portrait.

SINNOCK
(*pulling rank*) I am the Chief Engraver for the United States Mint, perhaps you don't understand how these things work.

SELMA
I understand that you are getting credit for my work.

SINNOCK
(*patronizingly*) Let me explain. The obverse portrait of the president is a composite of two studies which I made from life previously. I consulted many photographs, then I got *approval* from the Secretary of the Treasury –

SELMA

I don't care if you got approved by every other white man in the government. We both know that the J.S. should be S.B. You will publicly acknowledge this with a press conference and an article of admission for *The Wall Street Journal.*

SINNOCK

(*beat*) I am not inclined to do that.

SELMA

And I am not inclined to let you get away with this!

SINNOCK

It's already been minted. (*chortling*) Are you going to go up to every man on the street, demand to see his pocket change, snatch it away, and re-engrave each one? How fanciful and amusing you are.

SELMA

How immoral and thieving you are.

SINNOCK

Yours was just one of many images I sourced, and as it says on the reverse – E Pluribus Unum – "Out of Many, One."

SELMA

And as it says on the obverse, "In God We Trust." I trust God will send you to hell.

SCENE 20

Three Files and an Offer

FBI field office, New York. SELMA is waiting in an empty office. She looks out the "window."

SELMA
Hey, Lady Liberty!

Lady LIBERTY comes into view.

LIBERTY
Hey, Selma!

SELMA
I wonder if J. Edgar Hoover will want his statue to be as big as you!

LIBERTY
He has a big ego and a lot of power – he'll want his own Ellis Island!

SELMA
In your original model weren't you supposed to be holding the broken chain and shackle to represent our newly achieved freedom?

LIBERTY
Now they are at my feet.

SELMA
I wonder what Hoover will want to symbolize.

LIBERTY
He belongs to a southern fraternity set up after the defeat of confederacy, how can you immortalize him?

SELMA
But he fights corruption, fraud, vice, and pornography – people are complicated.

LIBERTY
You just came from the Pearl S. Buck House in Pennsylvania, maybe donate the commission there –

HOOVER enters, goes to his desk, and lays out three files, one white, one red, and one purple.

HOOVER
We wanted you to come in for a little chat.

SELMA
Great, we can chat as I sketch.

HOOVER
The Federal Bureau of Investigation is charged with protecting the law.

SELMA
I know.

HOOVER
We are a law enforcement agency. You are here for an investigation.

SELMA
(*beat*) You're investigating *me*?

LIBERTY
Run!

HOOVER
Have a seat.

SELMA
I don't understand –

SELMA sits.

HOOVER
One of the federal government's oldest agencies is the United States Mint.

SELMA
Oh. The Mint.

HOOVER
You gained unlawful admittance to a federal building and made charges against a federal employee of this agency.

SELMA and HOOVER stare at each other for a moment.

SELMA
So no commission. You tricked me.

HOOVER
It's just easier to have you come to the field office –

SELMA
It must be a slow day for crime if you're bringing me in.
I travelled back to New York, I'd say "on my own dime," but that would be a little too ironic, don't you think?

HOOVER
We respond to national security risks – you made threats against a government employee.

LIBERTY
Weasel Face –

SELMA
Sinnock.

HOOVER
You admit it.

SELMA

I admit I told him to go to hell.

HOOVER

We were going to let you off with a warning, however upon closer inspection we have discovered that you have been in the company of others known to us.

LIBERTY

Artists from the Harlem Renaissance? The president of the United States?

HOOVER

(*consulting his file*) Your associates seem to include known communist sympathizers.

SELMA

Claude is on the side of the workers in the struggle for fair pay and safe working conditions.

LIBERTY

Are fair pay and safe working conditions counter to the United States Government?

HOOVER

One of a twenty-two-person American *communist* delegation that travelled to *Russia* –

SELMA

And to England and Paris and North Africa –

HOOVER now gets out of his seat and towers over SELMA.

HOOVER

He is flagged in our Racial Matters Program –

SELMA

He *is* involved in racial politics –

HOOVER

With other communists, and the Red Threat in America is just as bad as the Lavender Threat. He's what we would call a (*beat*) Lavender Lad.

SELMA

Claude is –

HOOVER

He's a sexual pervert.

LIBERTY

So are you for taking the photos. I thought you were against pornography.

HOOVER

As well as being morally weak and psychologically disturbed, he undermines the traditional family. Security risk … susceptible to blackmail –

SELMA

No one would ever blackmail Claude, he never has any money.

HOOVER

Yes, he's always out of work because of his habitual drunkenness –

SELMA

He likes the occasional Jamaican rum.

HOOVER

And sexual perversion –

LIBERTY

Everyone needs a hobby.

HOOVER

And you, daughter of a preacher, are cavorting with this godless man. Do you want us to start a file on you too?

SELMA

If you know I'm the daughter of a preacher, you already have.

HOOVER

Elected officials come and go, but Hoover is the constant. Presidents in, presidents out, Democrats, Republicans. *Hoover* runs the USA. It wouldn't serve you well to disobey me.

HOOVER pulls out a newspaper clipping, casually.

Hey, this looks like you in this march.

LIBERTY

Somewhere I read of …

SELMA

The freedom of assembly. Somewhere I read of the freedom of speech. Somewhere I read that the greatness of America is the right to protest for rights.

HOOVER

(*menacingly*) Somewhere I read that J. Edgar Hoover *is* America.

SELMA

You're telling me to end my association with Claude?

HOOVER

It's in your best interests – you're not going to be making any more sculptures of presidents. (*sickly sweetly*) Of course, should you decide to help *protect* your country, you could report back to us with various information to pad out our files. Then we will find some lucrative commissions for you.

SELMA

I hope one day you can meet up with Sinnock in hell.

LIBERTY

Time to leave.

SELMA exits.

SCENE 21

Sparkler Art

A New York rooftop. It is night. A string of lights illuminates the skyline. We hear the faint hum of traffic in the background. SELMA looks out. MATISSE enters.

SELMA
No better place to see the Fourth of July than from a rooftop, Henri.

MATISSE
Bonjour, Selma.

SELMA
Your letter said you were coming, but you didn't say what you're doing in New York.

MATISSE
A commission for a mural.

SELMA
(*bantering good-naturedly*) If only they knew anyone more local –

MATISSE
You look, how you say? Stressed.

SELMA
My father just died.

SELMA holds out two sparklers and a lighter, and MATISSE positions the sparklers until they both light.

MATISSE
I'm so sorry, but he must have been proud of you –

SELMA

He thought I was a sinner.

SELMA and MATISSE "draw" in the air. MATISSE makes his famed leaf image; SELMA makes the outline of a body.

SELMA

He died alone. He still had the little face I carved for him in his pocket. He didn't know millions of my little faces are in everyone's pockets ... *and* I just got a call that one of my busts has been vandalized.

MATISSE

Non!

SELMA

It's not the first time. My work has been knocked down, vandalized ...

MATISSE

Félicitations!

SELMA

Congratulations? Why?

MATISSE

People don't destroy *benign* art.

SELMA

And most recently my art was stolen.

MATISSE

Stolen?! Did you report it to the police?

SELMA

It was stolen by the government.

MATISSE

People don't steal worthless art.

SELMA
Well, plagiarized ...

MATISSE
People don't reproduce bad art. Let's celebrate your success!

Fireworks explode, raining colour and sparkles down on them.

SCENE 22

Discrepancies with a Gavel

An auction house. NU DE DOS, QUATRIÈME ÉTAT, facing upstage, is being referenced by an auctioneer.

AUCTIONEER

(*voiceover with gavel bang*) Christie's, New York, sets a new record! Matisse's cast of his 1930 sculpture of a nude's back, *Nu de dos, quatrième état* at forty-eight point eight *million* dollars.

NU DE DOS, QUATRIÈME ÉTAT becomes GIRL, PRONE, and lights shift.

And here, *Girl, Prone,* by Selma Burke, sold for (*bang!*) fifteen *hundred* dollars.

SELMA enters. She is disappointed. HERMAN sidles over to SELMA, an auction catalogue in his hand.

HERMAN

I thought yours was worth more than his.

SELMA

Thank you.

HERMAN

I want to bid on this one.

HERMAN points to the statue, which has now become ISLAND DANCERS.

It's later on the docket.

SELMA
My *Island Dancers.*

She looks at the ISLAND DANCERS *slowly dancing. As the conversation progresses, the* ISLAND DANCERS *move slowly closer together until ultimately they are in an embrace.*

HERMAN
I've been following you ... (*catching himself*) as an artist for some time. That sounds creepy. But I'm a fan, a big fan of your work.

SELMA
Thank you.

HERMAN
You know, I always wanted to be an artist.

SELMA
Let me guess – your parents talked you out of it.

HERMAN
I still create things in a way.

SELMA
Yes?

HERMAN
I'm an architect. Herman Kobbe.

SELMA
I know who you are. You ran politically. You're a socialist, aren't you? I think some of my friends backed you.

HERMAN
I didn't win. Socialism has become a dirty word.

SELMA
Some of my best friends are socialists. My ex-husband was a communist.

HERMAN

I didn't see eye to eye politically with my ex-wife, either.

Pause.

SELMA

So, what are you building now?

HERMAN

I'm working on various projects ... I'd be happy to show you some of my blueprints?

SELMA

Is that the same as "Come up and see my sketches"?

HERMAN

(*laughing*) I'll buy you lunch first. You can tell me more about *your* next piece. Would it be forward of me to invite myself to your studio? I'd love to come and see your work.

SELMA

It's a very small studio.

HERMAN

I could build you a bigger one.

SELMA

I'd like to move away from the city, not retire but relocate to the country. I'll have to find a lot more buyers – not everyone is a fan like you. Herman.

HERMAN

How could anyone with a spark of feeling fail to love your work? Perhaps someday I could be of more help in other ways. Maybe fix up a fitting studio for you, with a garden and a bird bath and anything else you find necessary for your contentment.

SELMA looks at her watch, then at HERMAN.

SELMA

I'm free for lunch.

SCENE 23

Non Jamais

The art school. SELMA is chiselling away at the "NON JAMAIS" statue. CLAUDE enters, carrying his notebook. SELMA puts down her tools when she sees him.

SELMA
Claude!

CLAUDE
Hi Sel. I saw in the paper. You married the rich white man.

SELMA
No one has ever loved me the way he does.

CLAUDE
I loved you.

SELMA
In your way.

CLAUDE
Is he at home waiting for you by the fire?

SELMA
He's skiing in Vermont.

CLAUDE
Of course he is.

SELMA
I heard you were in Chicago?

CLAUDE

I was looking for a publisher for my new book *My Green Hills of Jamaica.*

SELMA

I haven't been a nurse for a while, but you don't look so good, baby.

CLAUDE

It's the dropsy.

SELMA

I thought they drained your heart last time you were in hospital.

CLAUDE

But my kidneys and ...

SELMA

Liver ... (*looking around*)

Pause.

CLAUDE

I always thought your work was good.

SELMA

No, you didn't.

CLAUDE

My favourite piece was *Light and Shadow*. The gold torso ... I never told you it was my favourite. I came here to tell you that.

SELMA

I assumed you're only here to "borrow" more money.

CLAUDE

You have everything, your degrees that people just hand you every time you turn around, awards, commissions, your art shows, your own school, must be nice.

SELMA
Claude, you lose your attractiveness when you're bittah.

CLAUDE
You could think more about supporting your community.

SELMA
And by "supporting my community" you mean "giving you more money"?

CLAUDE
You got your big shot politician, architect.

SELMA
Yes, he likes to build things up. You excel in tearing things down. You destroyed my clay. You smashed my maquettes. And over time you broke me.

Pause.

SELMA picks up her hammer and chisel and sets to work.

In appeasement, CLAUDE goes over to the "NON JAMAIS" statue she is working on. He sets down his notebook and takes a step back to give her new work a good look.

CLAUDE
You make nice decorative statues.

"NON JAMAIS"
Go to hell.

CLAUDE
I saw that the first time you showed me that little wooden carving of the mother holding her baby. It was very (*searching for the word*) maternal.

SELMA
Get out.

CLAUDE

It's a sweet, sentimental –

"NON JAMAIS"

Tell him.

As SELMA remembers, the MOTHER statue appears bathed in light.

SELMA

That depicted something *I lived through.* I'll never forget that moment in the dark, wet field. I was with our neighbour. She was protecting her baby after coming upon her husband's lifeless body, swaying from a lynching tree.

The MOTHER statue, facing upstage, reaches out her hand and lets out an anguished cry, seeing her husband.

CLAUDE

That's an important piece you made.

SELMA

I knew that sculptures could be more than art, they become *a record.* Her anguished face holding her son. Protecting him. After my bones turn to chalk, my statue of the two of them can still testify.

We hear a knock. The lights go down on the "NON JAMAIS" statue.

That will be my student here for her one-on-one lesson.

SELMA pulls herself together.

(*calling out*) Come in, Annette.

ANNETTE enters. SELMA goes to her purse, pulls out some bills, and hands them to CLAUDE. There is a moment. He thinks about kissing her on the cheek, doesn't. Inadvertently leaving his notebook behind, he exits.

ANNETTE
That was nice of you. You know, if you keep the school door locked, then beggars can't come in off the street.

SELMA
That wasn't a beggar. That was Claude McKay. One of this country's most gifted writers – a poet of the Harlem Renaissance.

ANNETTE
Oh.

ANNETTE goes to her backpack and gets a box.

I appreciate you taking me on, I'm having trouble, (*pulling out a sad-looking piece of clay*) it's always sculpted perfectly in my mind, it just comes out differently.

SELMA
You have to have patience with clay.

ANNETTE
I'm just not having a great day, I guess.

SELMA
Oh?

ANNETTE
Mommy is a liberal and said any artist who worked with FDR was good enough for her, but Daddy doesn't want me taking art classes. So, to get me to "reconsider my priorities" in life, he punished me by revoking my tennis membership at the club. This means I won't be able to attend the Christmas party, which I already have a new velvet dress for. It's midnight blue with willow pattern embroidery ... anyway, Jimmy won't get to see it.

He's my tennis coach, and I think he's sweet on me, although my friend Margery says he's sweet on *everyone*. But I love him.

SELMA
Well now, that *is* a problem.

ANNETTE
You're an artist, you even have your own art school. It must be nice to be old and not have these types of problems.

SELMA
I don't have those problems, Annette. I have problems finding time to come in here every day to wet the cloths to keep the clay pliable for students. I have students to find for classes, rent to pay on the studio. I have problems finding commissions that pay well, because Lord knows teaching won't keep the lights on. My last big commission fell through when I was lied to.
My problem is when I do busts of white folk, I get criticized for not promoting Black folk. When I do busts of Black folk, white folk don't buy them. When I do busts of ordinary folk, I am told serious artists only do famous folk. When I do famous folk, the ordinary folk complain I'm full of airs and graces. When I do celebrities, I get criticized for not immortalizing "serious people" like politicians. And when I do politicians, I'm accused of all sorts of things ...

When I create my own work, I'm told it's not like the work of Matisse. When I create work *exactly the same* as Matisse, I get told I'm "only copying the greats" and I'm "not an original."

You have your troubles with Jimmy the tennis coach, I got troubles with Jimmy the Crow. I got problems with segregation and discrimination. I got problems being told the only way to solve this is to march with people holding placards, who have marched so long they done wore out the soles of their shoes.
I got problems with white men who run the government, law enforcement, the courts – and one white man in particular who took credit for my portrait of the president of the United States. And when I complained, the FBI start investigating *me*. And this

morning when I came to open the studio, a young white boy spat on me and called me a n——.*

ANNETTE is aghast. Pause. SELMA looks at her "NON JAMAIS" statue.

"NON JAMAIS"
(*softly*) She's just a child, not all of that is her fault.

SELMA
(*realizing she has stepped over the line and trying to pull it back to teacher/student*) And you know the way I deal with my problems?

CLAUDE enters to retrieve his notebook. Unaware of him, SELMA crosses to the "NON JAMAIS" statue.

SELMA
I come to my studio, I pick up my hammer and chisel, and I try to carve out a better life for me and for my people, and I fashion for myself and others great, beautiful art for a world that's often ugly.

Face to face, locked in eye contact with her "NON JAMAIS" statue.

And when I show my beautiful art to the man that I loved, he says, "We shouldn't be making beautiful art, we should be making art that makes a difference."

Which brings me to my final and biggest problem, Annette – I don't know if my art makes a difference.

CLAUDE
(*softly*) It does.

---

* In performance the actor playing Selma should say the full word.

SELMA
Claude!

CLAUDE holds up his notebook as an explanation for his return.

ANNETTE
Oh, Miss Selma! I know how you can make a difference.

ANNETTE goes to her knapsack and pulls out a clipboard.

We are collecting signatures. The Social Justice Club at school is fighting racism, and we're collecting signatures. This will help.

SELMA
(*not unkindly*) No. It won't.

ANNETTE
Those Confederate statues that are in the southern states were put up for the glorification of war and justification for ... well, you know ...

SELMA
Go on ...

ANNETTE
(*hardly able to say the word*) Slavery. Some have already been vandalized and spray-painted by more radical groups, but *we* want to do it the ethical way. This is to pressure the state government to take them down. My daddy even signed it, and he's a conservative!

CLAUDE
And you want to put them in museums?

ANNETTE
Heavens, no! That would only make them more special – we want them melted down. You can sign it too, Mr. ...

CLAUDE

McKay. Claude McKay.

ANNETTE passes the petition to CLAUDE, and he signs, then holds it out to SELMA. SELMA looks at the paper and pen and then up at CLAUDE.

SELMA

It's still somebody's art.

CLAUDE

Those things aren't art, they are weapons of oppression and propaganda.

ANNETTE

Destroying them is the only solution.

Pause.

CLAUDE

If one of those men had lynched your neighbour, would you want to walk past it every day? Would you want her to see this constant reminder?

CLAUDE thrusts the pen and paper at SELMA, who doesn't take it.

ANNETTE

Come on. It's just a signature.

Long pause. SELMA turns to her "NON JAMAIS" statue, who holds up a hand in the swearing pose. She looks at him and the pose and turns to look at the other two.

SELMA

(*quietly, holding up her arm*) Non. Jamais.

CLAUDE

(*disgustedly*) Traitor.

SELMA

The solution is to reframe older art, recontextualize, dwarf it, make opposing art, make more art, make even *better* art.

"NON JAMAIS" nods in agreement.

SELMA

I'll fix this my way.

CLAUDE

Will the piece be political?

SELMA

Yes.

CLAUDE

In private collection?

SELMA

No.

CLAUDE

(*hopefully*) Will it be one of us?

SELMA

Yes.

CLAUDE

(*almost holding his breath*) Whose bust will it be?

SELMA

Not a bust, but a full-sized bronze.

SELMA tries out the pose.

He will reach out for something just beyond his grasp. He will have one foot as if climbing up.

CLAUDE
(*understanding*) Did he make it to the promised land?

SELMA
No. He looked over and he knew he wouldn't get there with us, but we know we as a people will get there.

CLAUDE
Not me.

SELMA
No, not us. Maybe your daughter.

CLAUDE
(*beat*) Hope.

Pause.

ANNETTE
I don't understand.

SELMA
(*directly to ANNETTE*) I know.

ANNETTE leaves, baffled. CLAUDE follows her out. SELMA picks up her chisel and hammer. She hits the chisel with the hammer. We hear the magnification of the sound of stone relenting and cracking. SELMA hits the stone again with more force; the noise is louder. She hits the stone again and again and again and the sound of stone breaking gets louder and louder and louder. The cracking swells into triumphant music. The lights fade on the stage, but then we see a shaft of gold light and standing in it is Dr. KING. SELMA drops her tools with a loud clang. She is spent.

SCENE 24

Guilt Reconciliation

Selma's studio apartment. PATSY is looking at SELMA, who is polishing Dr. KING's buttocks.

PATSY
Where did you get the human foot?

SELMA
I still have connections at the hospital.

PATSY
You stole human remains?!

SELMA
Can't steal what's already mine.

Pause.

PATSY
Yours?

SELMA
I own my body, I have a right to do with it what I will.

PATSY
That's not even true politically, much less legally.

SELMA
I didn't like the prosthetic the hospital issued, so I carved my own. Going to set my bones back inside it. Then I can sculpt myself whole again.

PATSY
You made your own leg?

SELMA

Who else knows it better than me? Well, I still have my vanity. I may have made the ankle a little slimmer.

SELMA reveals a white PLASTER OF PARIS LEG poking up from the plinth. It wiggles its ankle fetchingly.

PATSY

But you're not a doctor –

SELMA

I *am* a doctor. I was awarded eight PhDs and I *earned* two of 'em.

PATSY

But not in *medicine.*

SELMA

Leave. I have a deadline. The unveiling is tomorrow.

PATSY

Unveiling?

KING

You aren't the first to sculpt me –

SELMA

And I won't be the last – but you are *my* last.

PATSY

Won't be your last what?

KING

I suppose you think doing this work means something.

SELMA

It is something. Isn't that better than nothing?

PATSY

Who you talking to? It's either hallucinations or dementia. I'm calling the doctor, you sound unhinged.

PATSY exits.

KING

Are you unhinged, Selma Burke?

SELMA

Aren't all artists?

KING

You are the most eminent Negro sculptor in the USA.

SELMA

And you are the most eminent Negro ever.

KING

You won't ever be known. You'll never be adored like I was.

SELMA

At least I didn't get assassinated.

KING

No, you played it safe.

SELMA

(*softly*) Did I?

KING

And now I'm finished, and (*looking at her prosthetic*) you're finished.

SELMA

Yes. I usually do busts, it's a little strange to have to think about all of your anatomy.

KING
Well, it's been a while since I've been touched there ...

SELMA holds Dr. KING's face in her hand.

SELMA
And I got your jaw perfect.

KING
But there is something –

Dr. KING touches his face.

SELMA
There's something about your face ... not quite ...

KING
(*laughing*) I look a little like –

Dr. KING and SELMA face out as if to a mirror.

SELMA
Yes, I can see it too. I'm going to get criticized for that. Claude. Brilliant, talented, died without a dime to his name.

KING
You don't have a dime with your name.

SELMA flicks Dr. KING with her cloth.

SELMA
But – I'm worth quite a few dimes, and quarters, dollars too.

KING
And all before you married Herman –

SELMA
I can't believe I outlived three husbands.

KING
And one of 'em white!

SELMA
Yes, if Herman were Black, I'd still have him. White people, why do they got to go skiing? Black folk have bettah things to do than careen down a mountain with those fool things on. Fool gave himself a heart attack. That man had a big heart. I think it gave out because it was a little bit bigger than most.

PATSY re-enters holding an older mobile phone.

PATSY
Did you fall off the ladder at any point and hit your head?

SELMA
Don't keep interrupting me, woman. I'm in the presence of Doctor King!

PATSY
(*exits muttering*) I don't know. She thinks she's in the presence of a king ...

KING
Selma Burke, why *are* you doing this? You need to assuage your guilt?

SELMA
Maybe.

KING
I got the Nobel Peace Prize, what have you done with your life?

SELMA
I got some awards ... the medal President Jimmy Carter gave me in the Oval Office ...

KING
I hope one day we see a Black man sitting behind that desk.

SELMA

Not just any Black man. You paved the way for one that's noble, intelligent, kind, and leads with integrity. People tell me I should have held more signs. Signs come and go. They are usually made of cardboard. I've made you out of bronze, standing on marble.

I have a dream that maybe one day new art will pop up like flowers and populate all parks and streets and no one will see those other statues.

Pause. SELMA stands back to look at Dr. KING. He holds out his arms. They hug. All the tension seems to drain from SELMA. She stands back to look at him.

SELMA

(*sighing a big sigh*) Thank you, Reverend Doctor King.

KING

You've touched my butt – you can call me Martin.

SELMA gestures Dr. KING to his plinth. He puts one leg up. The lights shift and we transition to Marshall Park. It is a bright summer day. We hear park sounds and the sounds of a crowd. SELMA fashions Dr. KING's hand into the "Non Jamais" gesture and then extends the pose so that he is reaching out. The music swells as the lights go down on Dr. KING. SELMA remains in the spotlight; the music swells again. The lights go down on SELMA.

The End

SOURCES FOR QUOTED TEXT

SCENE 9

Selma's lines beginning, "I have not done this image for today ..." can be found in Karen D. Brame, *BLACKlisted Culture* (website), "Selma Burke," (1, no. 2) January 15, 2020, blacklistedculture.com/selma-burke.

SCENE 14A

Dr. King's lines beginning, "Somewhere I read of the freedom of assembly ..." are from his "I've Been to the Mountaintop" address delivered at Bishop Charles Mason Temple, Memphis, Tennessee, April 3, 1968.

SCENE 23

Herman's lines beginning, "How could anyone with a spark of feeling ..." quote a letter he wrote to Selma now held in the Selma H. Burke Papers collection in the Spelman College Archives in Atlanta, Georgia, Selma Burke part 1, box 2, n.d.

ACKNOWLEDGMENTS

This play was written and developed with generous assistance from the Alberta Foundation for the Arts, Calgary Arts Development, Spelman College Museum of Fine Art, Theatre Calgary, and Alberta Theatre Projects.

The playwrights wish to acknowledge the extraordinary support of Stafford Arima (artistic director, Theatre Calgary), Haysam Kadri (artistic director, Alberta Theatre Projects), and Dian Marie Bridge (artistic director, Black Theatre Workshop) for their invaluable assistance in the development of the script. Thanks also to Gerald Matthews, Hannah Kerbes, Ed Ogum, Elinor Holt, Doug McKeag, and Raynah Bourne. Big thanks also to Holly A. Smith, archivist at Spelman College, Atlanta, Georgia; the talents and time of brilliant sculptor Alexander Caldwell; and the creative Tara Blue for inside knowledge into living statues.

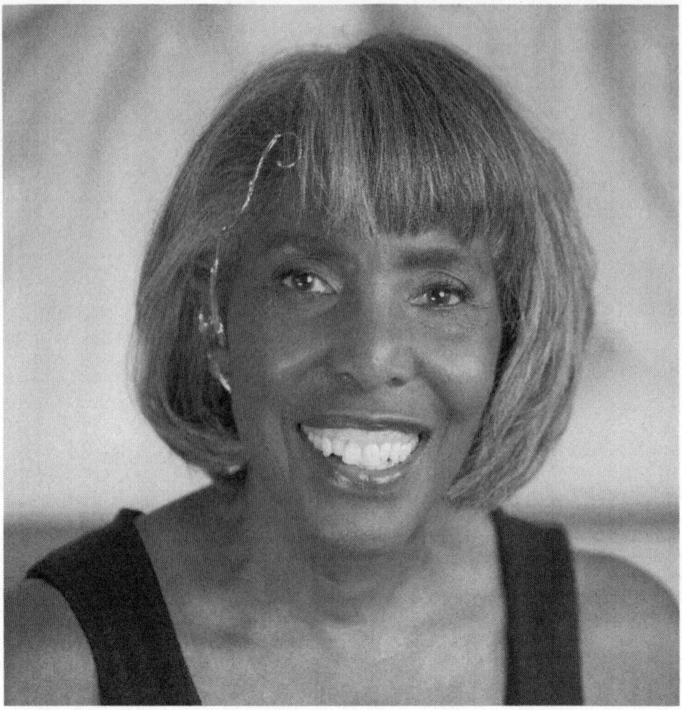

MARIA CROOKS, a Calgary playwright, has written full-length and one-act pieces. *Selma Burke: Carving a Sculptor's Life*, co-written with Caroline Russell-King, won the Betty Mitchell Award for Outstanding New Play, the Theatre BC Canadian National Playwriting Competition, and the Calgary Theatre Critics' Award for Outstanding New Play Script. It was a finalist for the Alberta Playwrighting Competition's Sharon Pollock Award. Her play *The Servant*, produced by Calgary's Urban Stories Theatre, was nominated for a CAT Award (Calgary Community Theatre Awards).
mariacrooks.com

PHOTO: BEN LAIRD

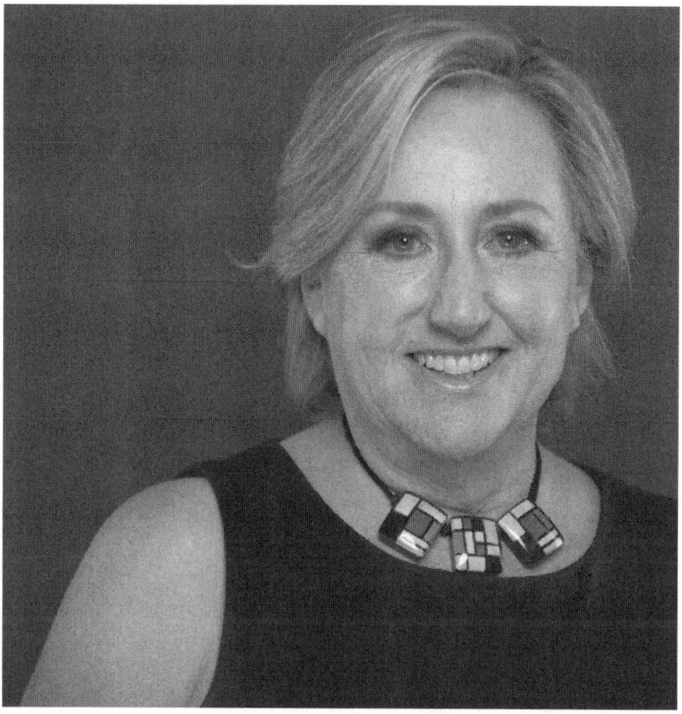

CAROLINE RUSSELL-KING is an award-winning playwright who has written thirty-three plays and had sixty-two productions across Canada and the USA. *Selma Burke: Carving a Sculptor's Life*, co-written with Maria Crooks, won the Betty Mitchell Award for Outstanding New Play, the Theatre BC Canadian National Playwriting Competition, and the Calgary Theatre Critics' Award for Outstanding New Play Script and was a finalist for the Alberta Playwrighting Competition's Sharon Pollock Award. Her play *High and Splendid Braveries* won the Writers' Guild of Alberta's Gwen Pharis Ringwood Award for Drama. Her work has been published in five anthologies, and her trilogy of comedy plays *Palliser Suite* was a finalist for the Stephen Leacock Medal for Humour. Nonfiction books include *Strategies: The Business of Being a Playwright in Canada* (with Rose Scollard) and *Do It Yourself Dramaturgy*. carolinerussellking.com

PHOTO: BEN LAIRD